A Concise History of Turkey: The History and Legacy of Turkey from Antiquity to Today

By Charles River Editors

Albor Zagros' picture of the ruins of the Gate of All Nations in Persepolis

About Charles River Editors

Charles River Editors is a boutique digital publishing company, specializing in bringing history back to life with educational and engaging books on a wide range of topics. Keep up to date with our new and free offerings with this 5 second sign up on our weekly mailing list, and visit Our Kindle Author Page to see other recently published Kindle titles.

We make these books for you and always want to know our readers' opinions, so we encourage you to leave reviews and look forward to publishing new and exciting titles each week.

Introduction

An ancient depiction of Persian Emperor Darius I

Lying in the middle of a plain in modern day Iran is a forgotten ancient city: Persepolis. Built two and a half thousand years ago, it was known in its day as the richest city under the sun. Persepolis was the capital of Achaemenid Persian Empire, the largest empire the world had ever seen, but after its destruction, it was largely forgotten for nearly 2,000 years, and the lives and achievements of those who built it were almost entirely erased from history. Alexander the Great's troops razed the city to the ground in a drunken riot to celebrate the conquest of the capital, after which time and sand buried it for centuries.

It was not until the excavations of the 1930s that many of the relics, reliefs, and clay tablets that offer so much information about Persian life could be studied for the first time. Through archaeological remains, ancient texts, and work by a new generation of historians, a picture can today be built of this remarkable civilization and their capital city. Although the city had been destroyed, the legacy of the Persians survived, even as they mostly remain an enigma to the West and are not nearly as well understood as the Greeks, Romans, or Egyptians. In a sense, the Achaemenid Persian Empire holds some of the most enduring mysteries of ancient civilization.

Of course, one of the reasons the Persians aren't remembered like the Greeks is because of the way the Greco-Persian Wars ended. The Ancient Greeks have long been considered the forefathers of modern Western civilization, but the Golden Age of Athens and the spread of Greek influence across much of the known world only occurred due to the Greeks' victory in two of history's most important wars. In 491 BCE, following a successful invasion of Thrace over the Hellespont, the Persian emperor Darius sent envoys to the main Greek city-states, including Sparta and Athens, demanding tokens of earth and water as symbols of submission, but Darius didn't exactly get the reply he sought. According to Herodotus in his famous *Histories*, "Xerxes however had not sent to Athens or to Sparta heralds to demand the gift of earth, and for this reason, namely because at the former time when Dareios had sent for this very purpose, the one people threw the men who made the demand into the pit and the others into a well, and bade them take from thence earth and water and bear them to the king."

Thus, in 490 BCE, after the revolt in Ionia had been crushed, Darius sent his general Mardonius, at the head of a massive fleet and invading force, to destroy the meddlesome Greeks, starting with Athens. The Persian army, numbering anywhere between 30,000 and 300,000 men, landed on the plain at Marathon, a few dozen miles from Athens, where an Athenian army of 10,000 hoplite heavy infantry supported by 1,000 Plataeans prepared to contest their passage. The Athenians appealed to the Spartans for help, but the Spartans dithered; according to the Laws of Lycurgus, they were forbidden to march until the waxing moon was full. Accordingly, their army arrived too late. Thus, it fell upon the Athenians to shoulder the burden. With their army led by the great generals Miltiades and Themistocles, the Athenians charged the outnumbering Persians. Outmatched by the might of the heavy, bronze-armored Greek phalanx, the inferior Persian infantry was enveloped and destroyed, causing them to flee for their ships in panic. The Athenians had won a colossal victory against an overwhelming and seemingly invincible enemy.

Darius's son and successor, Xerxes, would fare no better. When the Spartans' famous and sacrificial stand at the Battle of Thermopylae ended, the Athenian fleet was forced to fall back, and Xerxes's massive Persian army marched unopposed into Greece before advancing on Athens. The Greek armies were scattered and unable to face the might of Persia, so Athens was forced to do the unthinkable: evacuate the entire population of the city to Salamis, from where the Athenians watched in horror as Xerxes's troops plundered the defenseless city, set it aflame, and razed the Acropolis.

However, the Athenians remained belligerent, in part because according to the oracle at Delphi, "only the wooden wall shall save you." Indeed, this would prove true when Themistocles managed to lure the Persian fleet into the straits of Salamis. There, on a warm day in September

480 BCE, hundreds of Greek and Persian ships faced each other in a narrow strait between the Attic peninsula of Greece and the island of Salamis. The battle that ensued would prove to be epic on a number of different levels, as it set a precedent for how later naval battles were fought in the ancient Mediterranean, turned the tide in the Greeks' favor against the Persians in the Persian Wars, and ultimately played a role in Athens' rise to a preeminent role in the Hellenic world.

In terms of geopolitics, perhaps the most seminal event of the Middle Ages was the successful Ottoman siege of Constantinople in 1453. The city had been an imperial capital as far back as the 4th century, when Constantine the Great shifted the power center of the Roman Empire there, effectively establishing two almost equally powerful halves of antiquity's greatest empire. Constantinople would continue to serve as the capital of the Byzantine Empire even after the Western half of the Roman Empire collapsed in the late 5th century. Naturally, the Ottoman Empire would also use Constantinople as the capital of its empire after their conquest effectively ended the Byzantine Empire, and thanks to its strategic location, it has been a trading center for years and remains one today under the Turkish name of Istanbul.

The end of the Byzantine Empire had a profound effect not only on the Middle East but Europe as well. Constantinople had played a crucial part in the Crusades, and the fall of the Byzantines meant that the Ottomans now shared a border with Europe. The Islamic empire was viewed as a threat by the predominantly Christian continent to their west, and it took little time for different European nations to start clashing with the powerful Turks. In fact, the Ottomans would clash with Russians, Austrians, Venetians, Polish, and more before collapsing as a result of World War I, when they were part of the Central powers.

The Ottoman conquest of Constantinople also played a decisive role in fostering the Renaissance in Western Europe. The Byzantine Empire's influence had helped ensure that it was the custodian of various ancient texts, most notably from the ancient Greeks, and when Constantinople fell, Byzantine refugees flocked west to seek refuge in Europe. Those refugees brought books that helped spark an interest in antiquity that fueled the Italian Renaissance and essentially put an end to the Middle Ages altogether.

In the wake of taking Constantinople, the Ottoman Empire would spend the next few centuries expanding its size, power, and influence, bumping up against Eastern Europe and becoming one of the world's most important geopolitical players. It was a rise that would not truly start to wane until the 19th century.

The long agony of the "sick man of Europe,"[1] an expression used by the Tsar of Russia to depict the falling Ottoman Empire, could almost blind people to its incredible power and history. Preserving its mixed heritage, coming from both its geographic position rising above the ashes of the Byzantine Empire and the tradition inherited from the Muslim Conquests, the Ottoman

Empire lasted more than six centuries. Its soldiers fought, died, and conquered lands on three different continents, making it one of the few stable multi-ethnic empires in history, and likely one of the last. Thus, it's somewhat inevitable that the history of its decline is at the heart of complex geopolitical disputes, as well as sectarian tensions that are still key to understanding the Middle East, North Africa and the Balkans.

When studying the fall of the Ottoman Empire, historians have argued over the breaking point that saw a leading global power slowly become a decadent empire. The failed Battle of Vienna in 1683 is certainly an important turning point for the expanding empire, as the defeat of Grand Vizier Kara Mustafa Pasha at the hands of a coalition led by the Austrian Habsburg dynasty, Holy Roman Empire and Polish-Lithuanian commonwealth marked the end of Ottoman expansionism. It was also the beginning of a slow decline during which the Ottoman Empire suffered multiple military defeats, found itself mired by corruption, and had to deal with the increasingly mutinous Janissaries (the Empire's initial foot soldiers).

Despite it all, the Ottoman Empire would survive for over 200 more years, and in the last century of its life it strove to reform its military, administration and economy until it was finally dissolved. Years before the final collapse of the Empire, the Tanzimat ("Reorganization"), a period of swiping reforms, led to significant changes in the country's military apparatus, among others, which certainly explains the initial success the Ottoman Empire was able to achieve against its rivals. Similarly, the drafting of a new Constitution (*Kanûn-u Esâsî*, basic law*)* in 1876, despite it being shot down by Sultan Abdul Hamid II just two years later, as well as its revival by the "Young Turks" movement in 1908, highlights the understanding among Ottoman elites that change was needed, and their belief that such change was possible.

Looking at the events of the empire's last two centuries, and interpreting the fall of the Ottoman Empire as a slow but long decline is what could be called the "accepted narrative." At the start of World War I, the Ottoman Empire was often described as a dwindling power, mired by administrative corruption, using inferior technology, and plagued by poor leadership. The general idea is that the Ottoman Empire was "lagging behind," likely coming from the clear stagnation of the Empire between 1683 and 1826. Yet it can be argued that this portrayal is often misleading and fails to give a fuller picture of the state of the Ottoman Empire. The fact that the other existing multicultural Empire, namely the Austro-Hungarian Empire, also did not survive World War I should put into question this "accepted narrative." Looking at the reforms, technological advances and modernization efforts made by the Ottoman elite between 1826 and the beginning of World War I, one could really wonder why such a thirst for change failed to save the Ottomans when similar measures taken by other nations, such as Japan during the Meiji era, did in fact result in the rise of a global power in the 20th century.

During the period that preceded its collapse, the Ottoman Empire was at the heart of a growing rivalry between two of the competing global powers of the time, England and France. The two powers asserted their influence over a declining empire, the history of which is anchored in Europe as much as in Asia. However, while the two powers were instrumental in the final defeat and collapse of the Ottoman Empire, their stance toward what came to be known as the "Eastern Question" – the fate of the Ottoman Empire – is not one of clear enmity. Both England and France found, at times, reasons to extend the life of the sick man of Europe until it finally sided with their shared enemies. Russia's stance toward the Ottoman Empire is much more clear-cut; the rising Asian and European powers saw the Ottomans as a rival, which they strove to contain, divide and finally destroy for more than 300 years in a series of wars against their old adversary.

Last but not least, the rise of nationalism among peoples under Ottoman domination was a key factor in the dissolution of the empire. At the end of the 19th century, shortly before its final collapse, the territory of the Ottoman Empire dwindled due to the growing call for independence coming from different ethnicities it ruled for hundreds of years. The Empire's inclusiveness, which marked it as a direct successor of the Byzantine Empire, was most certainly challenged by an aging leadership. The Ottoman Empire's inability to create a shared identity, a weak central state, and growing inner dissensions were some of the main factors explaining its long demise. Such a failure also explains the need for the creation of a new form of identity, which was ultimately provided by Mustafa Kemal, the founding father of modern Turkey.

Overall, the history of the dissolution can be defined as a race between the Empire's growing "illness" on one side (the Ottoman's inability to appease and federate the various people within its territory), and constant attempts to find a cure in the form of broad reforms. These questions are often presented together, but that tends to shift the focus outward, onto the various peoples and their aspirations, along with Europe's growing influence over the fate of the Ottoman Empire. To consider both the "illness" and the cure, it's necessary to separate them, before moving on to the direct cause of the empire's dissolution (World War I) and its heritage.

A Concise History of Turkey: The History and Legacy of Turkey from Antiquity to Today provide a brief but comprehensive overview of Turkey over the past 3,000 years. Along with pictures depicting important people, places, and events, you will learn about Turkey like never before.

A Concise History of Turkey: The History and Legacy of Turkey from Antiquity to Today

About Charles River Editors

Introduction

Ancient Anatolia

The standard encyclopedia definition of "Anatolia" (known also as Asia Minor or the Anatolian Plateau) describes a peninsular of land defining the westernmost protrusion of Asia. More than two-thirds of modern Turkey comprises the Anatolian Plateau, which, besides its many human and geographic fascinations, places modern Turkey precisely at the crossroads between the East and the West. It is this unique position that has shaped and defined both the ancient and modern history of this unique nation, and, no doubt will continue to do so.

The character of Anatolia, as a distinct region, and as its name implies, is that of a high plateau extending from the steppes of Central Asia to the coast of the Aegean, bordered to the east by the hills and mountain chains of Armenia, to the south by the rugged Taurus Mountains and to the north the Black Sea. The former serves as a natural barrier between Turkey and Iran and the latter between Turkey and the low-lying regions of Syria and Iraq. To the west, smaller mountain ranges that run east to west plunge into the Aegean Sea, surfacing periodically as the Greek islands. The Black Sea is linked to the Aegean via the Sea of Marmara, the Bosporus and the Straits of the Dardanelles.

Asia Minor forms something of a northwestern extension to the region known Mesopotamia, broadly between the Tigris and the Euphrates, which is today regarded as the "Cradle of Civilization." Here was the first human transition from the nomadic lifestyles of the hunter-gatherer to the settled conditions of agricultural and pastoral styles of life. Although the first evidence of human habitation on the Anatolian Plateau can be reasonably accurately dated to the Paleolithic Period (500000–12000 BCE), the first settled human societies practicing agriculture and animal husbandry begin to appear only during the Neolithic Period, beginning at around 10000 BCE. This is what archaeologists now refer to as the "Neolithic Revolution," a great leap forward in human evolution that set in motion the long march towards human civilization as we recognize it today. It is extraordinary to imagine that that visible antiquities of modern Turkey, Iraq and Iran are overlaid upon even more ancient layers of human civilization, lost in an era of prehistory before written chronicles and with just the scantest surviving archaeological record.

The Eastern Mediterranean and the expanses of Asia Minor have been the subject of intensive and ongoing archaeological work since the early Victorian Era. One of the most extensive and best preserved Neolithic settlements to be discovered during this period was *Çatal Höyük*, located in the southern Anatolian region, southeast of the modern city of Konya, and which has since fascinated generations of archaeologists. Interest in the site was prompted by the British amateur archaeologist David George Hogarth, a contemporary of another great scholar, Orientalist and soldier, Thomas Edward Lawrence. Hogarth made note of a local legend claiming that Konya was the first human settlement of any size to emerge after the great flood.[2] The site

---

[2] Readers should note that the Hebrew legend of the flood places the final resting place of Noah's Ark on Mount Ararat, part of the Armenian range at the eastern extremity of Turkey.

upon which the settlement was built lies on the edge of an ancient lake, which might perhaps have been the source of the legend, but at the very least, the alluvial deposits left behind by the receding waters were sufficiently fertile to support what became, in practical terms, the first known human city.

The site is extensive, covering some thirty-two acres, and its civic architecture comprised simple, single-story mud-brick structures, mostly domestic dwellings, which were built in a manner that suggests the need not only for shelter but also defense. The economy of the settlement was primarily centered around agriculture, but local deposits of obsidian were also important for the manufacture of tools and implements, before the development of iron, and representing the first items of prehistoric trade. Another unique and interesting feature of *Çatal Höyük* is the number of mural paintings that survive, depicting scenes of both religious significance and nature, and featuring both local wildlife and landscape. There is, for example, a well-known depiction of the eruption of *Hasan Dağı*, a twin-summited volcano to the east of Konya, with the city of *Çatal Höyük* featured in the foreground.[3]

Çatal Höyük survived as a coherent site of human habitation for a little under 2,000 years, reaching its peak in about 7000 BCE and disappearing from the archaeological record in about 5700 BCE. By the advent of the Bronze Age, however, the region of Anatolia had come to be characterized by quite a number of well-established and fortified city-states, including Troy, Poliochni on the Greek island of Lemnos, Beycesultan, located in western Anatolia, Boğazkale, a fortified mound in central Anatolia, and Alaca Höyük in north-central Anatolia.[4] These sites all represent well-established societies of both artistic and technical accomplishment, but about the identity and racial affinities of the inhabitants, nothing at all is known. The advent of metalworking technology, dated also from about this time, obviously added much to the prosperity of traditionally agricultural societies, as did long-distance trade between Anatolia and Mesopotamia, which can be dated as early as 2600 BCE.

The Middle Bronze Age, at last, brings the region of modern Turkey into the era of proto-history, which is thanks mainly to the observations and cuneiform writing of the neighboring Assyrians. These written records were related almost entirely to trade, which appears to have been mainly in the importation into Syria of Anatolian iron, gold and silver, and perhaps also obsidian, rock-crystal and glazed pottery. The Anatolian trade centers, however, appear to have made no use of written text in any form, and what information is available originates entirely from the Assyrians. Trade, however, was sophisticated, and the centers of trade comparatively prosperous. Anatolian religion was naturalistic, which was commonly the case at the time, focusing on the elements of nature – the sun, the moon and the planets – on figurines of bulls and stags, and on a mother-goddess known as Kubabat, and later in the Greek, as Cybele.

---

[3] There is considerable controversy surrounding this depiction, and its interpretation, which some references suggest was an early map.

[4] The present-day name for the site of Troy is Hisarlik, located at a point just south of the entrance to the Dardanelles

The first identifiable period of dynastic succession and imperial rule began in about 2000 BCE, with the advent of the Hittites.

With the Hittites there also came written language, which at last projects the region of Asia Minor out of the obscurity of proto-history into the much better illuminated era of recorded history. It now becomes possible to plot, in far greater detail, the rise and fall of empires and the development of human society. The Hittites dominated the region of Anatolia for most of the second millennium BCE, which was an age of enormous development and change, spanning the important transition between the Middle and Late Bronze Ages. Human society entered upon a period of rapid development and diversification, and while the first half of the millennium was dominated by the Middle Kingdom of Egypt and Babylonia, the second saw the rise of the Minoan Greeks of the Aegean and the Hittites of Anatolia. By the end of the millennium, bronze had transitioned to iron, which triggered the great leap forward witnessed across the gamut of what is now regarded as the Cradle of Civilization.

The origins of the Hittites, despite the expanding archaeological record, remains somewhat obscure, although the most commonly accepted theory is that they began appearing in Anatolia around 2000 BCE from the Caucasus region, responding perhaps to some sort of turmoil in that region. Their takeover was gradual and bloodless, and they rose to dominate the indigenous Hatti people of Anatolia as the natural progression of a ruling aristocracy, borrowing much in terms of language and culture. The early kings of the Old Kingdom consolidated and then extended Hittite control over most of Anatolia and large areas of what is today northern Syria. King Mursilis I, who reigned from approximately 1620-1590 BCE, pushed the boundaries of the empire down the Euphrates River as far as the ancient Amorite city of Babylon. The New Kingdom, regarded now as a fully-fledged empire, is dated between 1400 and 1200 BCE.

The Hittites featured widely in the Old Testament as the enemies of the Israelites and despisers of the God Jehovah. According to Genesis 10, they were the descendants of Heth, the son of Canaan, who was the son of Ham, born of Noah. The first successful development of iron metallurgy as a human craft is often attributed to the Hittites, and they were among the first to make effective use of chariots in battle. The most notable military achievement of the Hittites was the Battle of Qadesh (1286 BCE), fought between Muwatallis, who ruled the empire from 1320-1294 BCE, and Ramses II of Egypt. This is today regarded as one of the largest and most significant battles of the ancient world. Hittite religious practices varied significantly across the geographic scope of the empire, although in detail it appears that religious ritual and practice were a continuation and development of earlier cults centered around a mother goddess, in which worship was offered to the natural elements. The king enjoyed divine status. Surviving Hittite art tends to be flat and two-dimensional, and without particular flair, and beyond the record of prayers and ceremonies, there was little if any literature.

The empire of the Hittites began to fall into decline at the end of the second millennium, by the last century of which it had broken up. Through the Classical era, minor Hittite dynasties survived, merging ultimately into the modern demographic of the Levant.

The fall of the Hittites, in the meantime, saw the rise of the kingdoms of Phrygia and Lydia, both during the Classical period, and indeed it was these two kingdoms that faced the rise of Greek civilization across the Aegean as it began to flourish and prosper. Alexander the Great, according to legend, cut the Gordian Knot in the Phrygian capital of Gordium when challenged by the citizens to separate it. According to Homer's Iliad, the Phrygians participated in the Trojan War as allies of Troy, and it was under the legendary King Midas, he of the golden touch, that the empire reached its greatest extent.

The history of both Phrygia and Lydia falls in an age that is regarded as the "Dark Age" of Anatolian history, and of the history of Western Asia in general, for within this span the archaeological record falls inexplicably silent, and very little is heard. The Phrygian empire emerged in the eighth century BCE, originating, as the early Greeks believed, from south-eastern Europe. By the end of the eighth century, as the curtain of the Dark Ages begins to be drawn, the Phrygians were in their death throws, displaced by the Cimmerians of southern Russia, who sacked the city of Gordium in 714 BCE.

As the Phrygians faded from the picture, however, the Lydians emerged, a stronger and somewhat more enduring empire. The Lydians were probably related to the Hittites, and by the second millennium, they were established in Asia Minor as a powerful kingdom. Like the Phrygians, they were pruned back somewhat by the Cimmerian invasion but were then revived in the aftermath in a more substantial form. According to Herodotus, the Lydian Candaules, so admiring of the beauty of his wife, offered his favorite minister Gyges the opportunity to spy on her naked body. Gyges took the opportunity but was caught, and so compromised was he that he was threatened with death. The queen then offered him the choice between his own death and killing Candaules and founding a new dynasty. Unsurprisingly, Gyges chose the latter and duly founded the Mermnad dynasty of Lydian kings.

The Lydian Empire was an iron-age kingdom, and its center can perhaps be pinpointed as ancient Ionia, a region of the west coast of modern Turkey, close to the city of İzmir. It existed from about 1200-546 BCE, and at its greatest extent it covered all of western Anatolia. Ionian society achieved an extremely high level of cultural sophistication, prospering and developing on the edge of the great intellectual and cultural achievements underway in Greece, and reflected in the wider region of the Eastern Mediterranean and Western Asia. Philosophy, poetry, art and architecture all flourished, often undisturbed by momentous political events that were beginning to take place around them. Those events pertained to the Persian invasion, another of the great permutations of Western Asian history. This process was completed in 547 BCE by the final conquest of Lydia, and with the occupation of the Lydian cities of Ionia and Lycia, Persian Rule was established throughout Asia Minor.

The Achaemenid Empire

Thereafter, Lydia became a province of the Achaemenid Persian Empire. The administrative division of the Achaemenids was the satrapy, and the satrapy of Lydia was ruled, as was every similar province, by a satrap (governor), appointed by the central Persian rulers. All of the regions of Anatolia were similarly absorbed, organized and governed.

It is worth noting here that among the larger and more important satrapies of eastern Anatolia was the Satrapy of Armenia, derived from the Orontid dynasty, a hereditary Armenian line of succession originating from the Iron Age kingdom of Uratu. The Orionids emerged as a regional power at around the time of the Scythian and Median invasions of the sixth century BCE.

The Achaemenid Empire existed between 550 and 330 BCE, growing at its greatest extent to include Asia Minor, most of Western Asia and regions of the Lower Nile. Also known as the First Persian Empire, it was centered in modern-day Iran and was the largest empire ever established up to that time. Much of the reason for the success of Achaemenids was the standardization of administration and language across the entire reach of the empire, and the centralization of government using the system of provinces governed by appointed regional governors. A professional, uniform civil service and a standing army were also rather advanced imperial principles that were applied universally by the Achaemenids. Perhaps the most famous of Achaemenid supreme rulers was Darius I, or Darius the Great, grandson of the founding ruler Cyrus. Darius was the one perhaps most responsible for the advances in organization, communications and government that so characterized the empire. It is also interesting to note that Achaemenid ruling elites in the provinces tended to retain their exclusivity in just a few households, exerting ultimately very little influence over the arts, culture and religion of the subject regions. It was thanks to this that the classical culture of old Lydia, centered around the city of Ionia, survived the change of imperial rule without major modification.

A relief at Behistun depicting Darius

Anatolia was nonetheless an important region of the empire. In a major advance during his reign, Darius I ordered the construction of the Royal Road, linking the Persian city of Susa, just east of the Tigris River near its outflow into the Persian Gulf, to the western Anatolian coastal city of Sardis. While Persian rule over Anatolia was stable, ordered, peaceful and reasonable, satrapies did periodically revolt, and thus, the early fifth century BCE saw a handful of Ionian cities do precisely that.

The Ionian Revolt of 499 BCE proved to be an extremely important moment in the history of both the Eastern Mediterranean and Asia Minor, for it marked the moment of Greek resistance against Persian rule. It flared in association with a number of other related military uprisings in Aeolis, Doris, Cyprus and Caria, all of which were predominately Greek regions of Asia Minor. The Greeks referred to the satraps in their own parlance as "tyrants," and it was the dissatisfaction with a handful of individual tyrants appointed by the Persians that prompted a coordinated rebellion. In in the wider scope of the revolt, the Ionians fought only one major battle, the Battle of Ephesus, which they lost, and after which they adopted a largely defensive posture. By 493 BCE, the Persians had regained control of what were their most important outer provinces, and Ionia was served articles of peace that have historically been regarded as both fair and lenient.

Nonetheless, the entire episode was important simply because it marked the effective commencement of the Greco-Persian Wars, which in turn served as a backdrop to one of the greatest military epics of history. While Asia Minor had been effectively returned to the fold, Darius was nonetheless determined to punish Athens and Eretria for their open support of the revolt, and moreover, sensing the rising power of the many Greek city-states as a growing threat to the empire, he took the decision to conquer Greece in its entirety. As a direct consequence of the Ionian Revolt, which set the whole process in motion, the first Persian invasion of Greece began in 492 BCE.

The culmination of Darius's campaign was the defining battle fought at Marathon between a vast Persian army and the much smaller army of Athens. The battle resulted in an unexpected Athenian victory, which not only put an end to Darius's Greek adventures but also gave Athens a commanding, albeit unpopular leadership position among the Greeks. This was resented most acutely by Athens' main rival, the city-state of Sparta. As far as Anatolia was concerned, it lay somewhat outside the main theater of these events, and as a consequence, the first part of the fifth century was a period of relative peace and stability, as these momentous events roiled around it.

Darius, in the meanwhile, died in 485 BCE and was succeeded by his son Xerxes, who very quickly realigned himself with the strategy of Greek conquest, and before long another massive army was on the move. In the spring of 480 BCE, the Persian army reached Hellespont at the mouth of the Dardanelles, and from there it marched resolutely into Europe. The Spartans were well defeated at the Pass of Thermopylae, and after a siege of two weeks, the invaders sacked the city of Athens in an orgy of violence lasting two weeks. The Athenians, however, counter-attacked on water, and at the Battle of Salamis the Persian fleet was destroyed. Xerxes was advised to evacuate, and he did, leaving the field to his chief military commander Mardonius, who was again comprehensively defeated by a combined Greek force at the Battle of Plataea, followed by a second naval defeat in the Battle Mycale.

A. Davey's picture of a relief depicting Xerxes on his tomb

A relief depicting a Persian king killing a Greek hoplite

The defeat at Mycale marked the end of any residual Persian ambitions to conquer Greece, and the demoralized Persian armies withdrew back into Anatolia, leaving the Greeks to plot their next move. This was an energizing and validating moment in Greek history, and the victors immediately established a confederacy to follow the retreating Persian across the Aegean to take the fight back to the mainland of Asia Minor. The Persian garrisons at Sestos, at the mouth of the Dardanelles, and at Byzantine, the future Constantinople, were expelled in 479 and 478 BCE respectively, and the Greeks thereafter established themselves in preparation for the next three decades, during which time all the Persian garrisons in Europe would be pushed back. Ionia was liberated in 466 BCE, although a series of major Greek reverses in Egypt then brought the Greco-Persian Wars to a quiet end.

The next event of significance to affect Asia Minor was a six-year episode known as the 'Great Satraps Revolt,' wherein several Anatolian satraps, ostensibly Loyal to Persia, rose in rebellion between 366 and 360 BCE. In brief, the satraps involved in the revolt were Datames, Ariobarzanes and Orontes of Armenia, and Mausolus, the Dynast of Caria, who were both for and against the Persians at different times. The rebellion, however, was put down by the Persians without any particular difficulty.

Then came the most momentous chapter of the great age of Greece. This was the brief era of Alexander the Great, who would emerge as the power that would expel the Persians from Asia Minor after an occupation of almost two centuries. The setting to this great episode of world history was the rise of the Macedon King Phillip II, a formidable figure eclipsed in the annals of history by his even more formidable son.

Alexander the Great and the Greeks

Giovanni Dall'Orto's picture of an ancient bust of Alexander

A bust of King Philip II of Macedon

In 336 BCE, Alexander's father, Phillip II of Macedon, was assassinated, and at the age of twenty, Alexander succeeded to the Macedon throne. For more than a century, the Greeks had lived under a self-imposed obligation to one day liberate the Greek cities of Asia and take revenge on the Persians for their invasion of Greece. The Macedonians, of course, were at best honorary Greeks, but nonetheless, Alexander took ownership of this objective and fixed his gaze east across the Aegean to the high plains of Anatolia. Within two years he secured his rear in Greece and Thrace, after which he gathered an army of some 50,000 men to march into Asia.[5]

He stepped on the continent of Asia Minor at Hellespont in the spring of 334 BCE and immediately made for Troy, and there he sacrificed to Athena of Ilium, and to the Greek heroes of war. Then, with scant time to spare, his conquest began. The Battle of the Granicus River was fought in May 334 BCE, the first of three major contests between him and the Persian army. At Granicus Alexander achieved an easy victory over a much larger army, after which he marched towards – and again easily took – Sardis. Ephesus, where he was to meet his fleet, he found abandoned by the Persian garrison. One by one, the other Greek cities offered their allegiance as the Persians rapidly rolled back. At Miletus, on the Aegean coast, the Persian fleet appeared to menace the much smaller Greek fleet, but Alexander simply took the city while declining to

---

[5] *Thrace* was a historic region including the north shore of the Dardanelles and a wide area between the Black Sea and the Aegean Sea, comprising most of southern Bulgaria.

engage the enemy on water.

And so it continued. Every important city along the Aegean coast was taken while carefully avoiding any high-risk naval engagements. Turning inland, Alexander mopped up Phrygia, Cappadocia and finally Cilicia, before pausing at the foot of the Nur Mountains on the present-day Turkey-Syria frontier. There, however, he received the long-expected news that Darius III, the Persian ruler, was advancing across the plains of Issus, at the head of a vast army, to meet him. What followed was the Battle of Issus, perhaps the most defining action of Alexander's eastward march. About it, all that requires telling is that facing a force vastly superior in numbers, Alexander prevailed, thanks to a display of bold – indeed brilliant – strategy and decisive maneuvering. Darius suffered a humiliating defeat, after which he abandoned Anatolia, beginning a phase of the region's history known as the "Hellenistic Period." Alexander would go on to much greater adventure and far vaster achievement, but for the time being he consolidated his grip on the land of the future Turkey.

In just thirteen years of active campaigning, Alexander completely transformed and advanced the Greek world. A Greek caste now ruled from western Greece across an entire continent to central Asia. Alexander was proclaimed a god while the cult of his personality held the entire edifice together. Then, in June 323 BCE, Alexander died at the age of just thirty-three, probably of typhoid fever, leaving behind a dangerous power vacuum. His infant son and his mentally weak half-brother Arrhidaeus were placed in command of his empire, but this dual kingship had little hope of surviving. A series of wars inevitably followed: the Wars of the Diadochi, which, after two decades, settled the division of Alexander's empire, and quickly thereafter the Hellenistic world began to take shape. Among Alexander's surviving warlords, Craterus was named ruler of Macedon, Ptolemy of Egypt and Perdiccas and Antigonus of Asia.

In 301 BCE, the Battle of Ipsus was fought between members of this Diadochi to equalize the ambitions of the successors of Alexander the Great. The details of this battle are perhaps extraneous, suffice to say that it granted Ptolemy a part of southern Anatolia and most of Egypt and the Levant, which then combined to form the Ptolemaic Empire. Lysimachus, another Macedonian officer, and Diadochus became heir to western Anatolia and Thrace, while Seleucus, yet another Alexandrian general, albeit a minor figure in the pantheon of warlords, gained control of the rest of Anatolia, proclaiming it the Seleucid Empire.

The Seleucid Empire existed between 312 and 63 BCE, controlling a vast geographic area that stretched from the eastern Levant to the south shore of the Caspian Sea and as far east as the Indus River. The capital of the empire was established at Antioch, and a number of significant cities were constructed, among them Seleucia on Tigris and Seleucia in Pieria. While Macedon remained predominant in the affairs of the Greek Mainland, the two major powers remaining as a residue of Alexander the Great's vast conquest were the Ptolemaic and the Seleucid Empires, both of which would remain preeminent until the advent of Rome.

Seleucid died in 281 BCE, by which time, in any case, the Empire was coming under attack. Waves of Gaul were pressing down from the north, while to the east the King of Pergamon, Eumenes I, was asserting independence. In 246 BCE, Ptolemy led an invasion of the Seleucid Empire, successfully overthrowing a weak succession, and in 245 BCE he handed the lands of Phrygia to the king of the Hellenistic state of Pontus, surrounding the Black Sea, as a wedding present.

The Hellenistic era of Anatolian history, as was true across the Hellenistic world, tended to be one of cities, following the pattern of the Greek mainland. All of the rulers of the various kingdoms loyal to the Greek principle were also loyal to the notion of independent city-states. These city-states were typically characterized by individual codes of law and unique systems of government, which was very different from the previous Persian system of governed and standardized satrapies. It might, however, be worth noting that the western Anatolian satrapies tended to be less standardized and less loyal to central authority as the Persian empire aged. It was natural that societies on the western edge of Asia would be apt to look west rather than east, and as the influence of the Greeks grew, this increasingly became the case.

The economic basis of these cities, in the meanwhile, was usually agriculture, and although walled for defense, they were rarely capable of raising citizen armies, relying instead on the various kings and their mercenaries. These mercenaries, who were often ethnic Greek, were widely dispersed Anatolian shield, and as such acted as a medium for the spread of Greek culture.

Greeks and Greek society, although widely dispersed across Asia Minor during the Hellenistic period, also tended to be thin on the ground, and as a consequence, other, older styles of political unit existed alongside and in between the Greek pattern of city-states. Temple-states, for example, survived in pursuit of individual cults and were often granted guarantees of asylia, or inviolability and freedom from tax or tribute. These were often the site of festivals and games which ruling kings were invariably happy to support.

Despite similarities of government and law, however, few if any of the Greek cities of Asia Minor reached the same level of artistic and intellectual culture that so characterized the city-states, or poleis of ancient Greece, with perhaps the notable exception being the city of Alexandria in Ptolemaic Egypt. Alexandria, named after the original progenitor of the Hellenistic world, emerged as perhaps the most eminent center of culture and learning, attracting renowned scholars and writers from the earliest years of its creation. The closest that any poleis in Asia Minor reached to this level of distinction was Pergamon, a city in Aeolis, on the western edge of modern Turkey, seventy miles north of Izmir and sixteen miles from the coast of the Aegean. During the Hellenistic period, Pergamon emerged as the capital of the Attalid dynasty, active between 281 and 133 BCE, the kings of which transformed the city into one of a handful of notable cultural centers of the wider Greek world. The Book of Revelation makes reference to

Pergamon, in particular, the "Throne of Satan" or the "Great Altar," which was the centerpiece of a majestic and sprawling civic complex. Although very little of it remains standing today, at the height of Pergamum's prominence it was an artistically and technically accomplished edifice, comprising a theater, set in the hollow of a low hill alongside an extensive sanctuary and sprawling stadia and gymnasium.[6] The library, built during the reign of Eumenes II, closely emulates the Library of Alexandria, and it is said that when the contents were seized by Mark Anthony as a gift to Cleopatra it contained upwards of 200,000 volumes. The kings of Pergamon sponsored education at all levels, supporting a school of philosophy that, although perhaps not the most lustrous in the Greek world, was nonetheless eminent. Pergamon, however, was home to perhaps the most distinguished school of sculpture of the period (the Pergamene School), producing works that included the "Dying Gaul," the "Blade-Sharpener" and many other that later found their way into the collections of Roman aristocrats.

The Romans

Beginning in about the middle of the third century BCE, the Greek rulers of Asia Minor found themselves obliged to contend with the rise of a new power in the Eastern Mediterranean. Antiochus III's 192 BCE invasion of Greece was turned back at Thermopylae by the Roman General Manius Acilius Glabrio, and in 189 BCE the Galatians, a Gallic people of central Asia Minor, were subdued by the Roman consul Gnaeus Manlius Vulso, resulting in their abandonment of the ancient city of Gordium. Then, as a result of the decisive Battle of Pydna, fought in 168 BCE as part of the Third Macedonian War, the Romans consolidated their position in Greece, which was further cemented by the sack of Corinth in 146 BCE.

These events, taking place on the European mainland, convinced Attalus III, the last king of Pergamon, of the irreversible fact of Roman eastward expansion, and he bequeathed his kingdom to Rome, to which it passed upon his death in 133 BCE. This, in combination with the destruction of Carthage, on the south coast of the Mediterranean in the same year as Corinth, projected the Romans to mastery of the entire western Mediterranean. To the Greeks of the east, all of this was deeply alarming. Despite generations of warfare between the various kings, the Greeks had nonetheless acquired a standard of civilization that the Romans, aggressively militarist and focused on conquest, seemed to care little about. The Roman objective for the four centuries to follow was not to construct a great cultural edifice to rival the Greeks but to push the borders of their empire ever outwards, and in the East to the Euphrates and beyond.

However, as the Roman lyrical poet, Horace, remarked in 14 BCE, "*Graecia capta ferum victorem cepit et artes intulit agresti Latio.*"[7] Acknowledging the extraordinary cultural achievements of the Greeks, Roman poets and artists embarked on a systematic imitation of

---

[6] 'To the angel of the church in Pergamum write: 'I know your works, and where you dwell... where Satan's throne is. And you hold fast to my name, and did not deny my faith even in the days in which Antipas was my faithful martyr, who was killed among you, where Satan dwells.' *Revelation* 2:12

[7] Translation: *Greece, once conquered, herself conquered the artless victor, and planted the banner of civilization in the farmlands of Rome.*

Greek art, sculpture, literature, philosophy and architecture, creating the Roman classical style as an interpretation of the Greek. According to the British classical scholar Doctor Richard Stoneman, "The story of Roman rule in Asia Minor and the other lands of the East is in large part the story of the interplay between Roman methods of military rule, civic government and administration, and Greek and Near Eastern artistic and philosophical brilliance, allied to the heterogenous religious traditions of Greeks, Jews and Syrians."[8]

Across the empire, Roman cities were built along established Greek lines and utilizing Greek forms to produce a provincial architecture that would, in the end, be unique to Rome. Literature was produced in Greek, Latin and Hebrew, and religious synthesis and interaction between the two societies produced a pantheon of familiar cults and revelations, the most enduring of which, of course, was Christianity, the earliest roots of which were seeded in Asia Minor. It was, however, not just the Hellenistic world that found itself impacted in this way by the rudely aggressive advance of Rome, but also, further to the east, the kingdoms of Pontus and Armenia.

Pontus was an independent kingdom focused on the southern shore of the Black Sea between the Halys and Iris Rivers. It was reputed to have been founded by the first of six kings named Mithridates, who was a descendant of Darius the Great. The administration of the kingdom went on in the Persian tradition and was not thus directly part of the Hellenistic world. Mithridates VI, however, came into conflict with Rome over efforts to expand his kingdom, an event that triggered the Mithridatic Wars. While the details of this series of battles lie outside scope of this discussion, the result was nonetheless a ruthless campaign by the great Roman general Cornelius Sula, which ended in the defeat the Pontian king and his meek return to his own kingdom. His ambitions, however, were not quenched. Soon afterwards, the kingdom of Bithynia came under Roman control, and Mithridates took the opportunity to try and snatch it. The Romans returned, and again he was defeated, although this time the Romans sought to crush him completely. He resisted successfully, remaining in power within the limits of his kingdom. Later, it was the Roman general Pompey who took up the fight, pushing Mithridates all the way back on the Bosporus. As he did, he absorbed, although never quite pacified, the neighboring region of Armenia. The Kingdom of Pontus was inevitably absorbed as a Roman protectorate in 63 BCE, the same years that Mithridates died by suicide.

The Greek cities of Asia Minor, meanwhile, were absorbed into the Roman Empire piecemeal, and with a great deal less trauma and difficulty, and the wider region of Asia Minor was divided into the Roman provinces of Asia, Galatia and Cappadocia. A point of importance as we move on to the next era of the history of Asia Minor was the wide dispersal of Jewish communities throughout the region. Their numbers grew rapidly during the last century before the Common Era, retaining the privileges allotted them under the Seleucids. Their rejection of the Roman imperial cult, however, brought them into conflict with Rome, to the point, indeed, of rebellion, although in general they were respected and left to their own culture and religion.

---

[8] Stoneman, Doctor Richard. *A Traveler's Guide to Turkey*. (Interlink Books. New York. 1998) p74

The Byzantine Empire

One of the great moments of transition in history was the conversion of the Roman Emperor Constantine to Christianity, and his founding of the new Roman capital on the site of Byzantium, the future Constantinople. Moved by a vision of the cross during the 312 CE Battle of Milvian Bridge, Constantine made it his mission to convert the empire as explicitly and exclusively Christian.

At that time, the Church was riven with divisions over the matter of the Arian heresy. Upon this fractious dispute, Constantine imposed order by calling the first "Council of the Church," the Council of Nicaea, which sat in the spring of 325 CE. Besides imposing the Nicene Creed as the formal doctrine of the Church, Constantine declared himself its head, which thereafter fell under Roman administration, its hierarchy established upon the existing Roman administration. To every city was appointed a bishop, while Rome, Constantinople, Alexandria, Antioch and Jerusalem were granted the status of preeminent metropoles. Their Bishops of these cities were defined as patriarchs with regional jurisdictions, and the Church was officially exempted from taxation.

The founding of Constantinople, therefore, marked the commencement of the Christian era of Asia Minor. Constantine first named the city "New Rome," but its informal name of Constantinople gradually replaced the less regal original. Constantine, in the meanwhile, immediately set about fortifying and adorning his new capital.

A bust of Constantine

Constantine's reign lasted from 306-337 CE, and for the four decades or so that followed his death, the succession was disputed by his three sons, Constantine, Constans and Constantius. None, however, was able to achieve permanent and stable authority, and instead power passed to Julian, a cousin of all three, who thereafter became Emperor Julian II. During this period, the borders of Christendom were steadily pushed outward, although it was under Theodosius I, the last of the Roman emperors to rule over both the western and the eastern empires, that some of the greatest advances on behalf of Christianity were made.

It was Theodosius, for example, in 392 CE, who officially outlawed paganism throughout the empire, bringing an end, among a great many other changes, to the thousand-year tradition of the Olympic Games. Pagan temples were abandoned or repurposed, while the old festivals and ceremonies were gradually adapted to serve the needs of Christian worship. It was upon the death of Theodosius in 395 CE that the two empires, west and east, separated, divided between his sons Arcadius and Honorius, the latter assuming the purple of Byzantine.

Meanwhile, the Byzantine Empire remained primarily Greek-speaking, and the city of Constantinople remained its capital. The century or so that followed, in keeping with the

Christian advance, was characterized by ideological wars and battles against various heresies, and the more tangible threat of invasion by both the Persians in the east and the Slavic tribes of the Danube to the north. The growing authority of the Church in Rome, and the increasingly aggressive claims of the Pope caused at last a schism in the Church. The Eastern Church was formalized, and during the course of the fourth century, monasticism grew in scope and influence, spreading from Europe to Palestine and Syria, and eventually to Anatolia. The first convent in Constantinople was established by Isaac the Syrian during the reign of Theodosius, followed some six decades later by the Roman Studius, who founded the influential Basilica of Saint John, to which was also attached a monastery.

The end of the reign of the Emperor Justinian (527–567 CE) found the Byzantine Empire increasingly under siege. The invasions of the Slavs and Avar from the north was followed by the emergence of the Bulgars, north of the Danube River, who began aggressively pressing southwards. The greatest and most consistent threat during the turbulent reign of Justinian remained the Sassanian Empire of Persia. The Sassanians were the only imperial power capable at that time of seriously threatening the Roman Empire, and several legions permanently deployed to the eastern frontier to contain it. Although battles were regularly fought, the Persians were ultimately unable to secure any permanent territory west of the Euphrates, which then marked something of a boundary between the two empires. It was in the sixth century, however, that the two sides began to clash most aggressively over their common interest in controlling the territories surrounding the headwaters of the River Euphrates, an area between the Black and Caspian Sea. This comprised Armenia which existed as part of the Byzantine Empire, and Georgia, Iberia and Colchis, which remained within the Persian sphere of influence.

A mosaic of Justinian the Great

The region, however, was lawless and frequently disturbed by a brigand race known as the Tzani. Early in the reign of the Emperor Heraclius (610–641), as part of this ongoing contest for territory, Syria, Palestine, Egypt and North Africa were yielded by the Byzantines to the Persians. This was rather a serious setback, for it isolated Byzantine from its main source of grain, which was Egypt, triggering a crippling economic crisis. In the meanwhile, the Slavs and Avars continued to creep south, villagizing ruined and abandoned cities with agrarian hamlets, and dragging the once illustrious culture back centuries. In 626 CE, the Avars allied with the Persians to attack Constantinople itself, but under the Emperor Heraclius" command, and with a reorganized Byzantine army, the siege was lifted and the Persian army defeated at Nineveh.

This was a spectacular reversal of fortune, and the power of the Persians was effectively broken. However, as the dust was settling on the battlefield of Nineveh, a new, more dangerous threat had begun to build on the southeast horizon.

In the last eight years of his reign, Heraclius lost to the Arabs most of the provinces which he had delivered from the rule of the Persians. This was the commencement of the Arab-Byzantine

Wars, a series of wars and campaigns that went on between the seventh and eleventh centuries, between the mostly Arab forces of Islam and the Byzantine Empire.

The emergence as a major power of the Muslim Arab Caliphate, penetrating north from the Arabian Peninsular during the early decades of the seventh century, resulted in the rapid loss of most of Byzantine's southern provinces. Over the course of the next 50 years, under successive Umayyad Caliphates, steady attrition was wrought against the frontier of the Byzantine Empire, twice besieging Constantinople and seizing Byzantine regions of North Africa. After 718, and the second siege of Constantinople, the situation stabilized somewhat, and the Taurus Mountains, on the southern extremity of Anatolia, was established as the uneasy dividing line between the two empires and between the two religions.

The wars, however, did not stop, but continued for another four centuries, ebbing and flaring frequently across the informal frontier. In the tenth century, Byzantine broke through but was able to re-establish full control over northern Syria and Greater Armenia. The wars continued and the eleventh century was characterized by ongoing border conflicts along a line of separation that, despite these ongoing clashes, remained largely stable.

These ongoing military contretemps had also the effect of loosening the bonds of administered society. The colonate effectively disappeared, to be replaced by a freer peasantry engaged in a feudal relationship with large landowners.[9] The emergence of vast, landed estates throughout central Anatolia projected an aristocratic class into conflict with a narrowing bureaucratic elite now confined largely to Constantinople. Cities, standing once at the zenith of political power, shrank and were abandoned, and by the ninth century the harbor at Ephesus on the Ionian coast had silted up. Thus began a long period of decline.

In the meantime, the eighth century witnessed the rise of yet another attritive enemy pressuring the Empire from the north. These, of course, were the Bulgars, an Asiatic people originating from the lands around the Volga River on the north shore of the Caspian Sea. Related closely to the Huns, they gradually settled the region today known as Bulgaria, coming increasingly into conflict with the Byzantine Empire as early as the late fifth century. By the end of the seventh century, they were settled south of the Danube, and in 809 they took the key Byzantine stronghold of Sardica.

Meanwhile, the Arab attacks, while challenging Byzantine control at the edges of the Empire, also had the effect of loosening the Byzantine grip on Armenia, over which the Arabs established only nominal control. The Armenians largely held out in their hills and mountains while the Arabs surrounded them. This had the effect of creating among the Armenians a distinct national consciousness which they had not experienced since the era of Tiridates. The Armenians had by then already made their mark at the center of the Empire, including contributing more than one

---

[9] *Colonate* - A peasant class of Ancient Rome which was legally tied to the land but could not be bought or sold.

emperor and at least a patriarch. And while the Armenians may have been practically besieged by Arabs, they were nonetheless willing to trade and interact with them, and a great deal of independent wealth and influence accrued in Armenian society. During the course of the ninth and tenth centuries, several Armenian dynasties emerged, and by the end of the tenth century, Armenia existed as a powerful, prosperous and independent kingdom. While the Caliphs displayed goodwill towards the Armenians, perhaps making a virtue out of necessity, strife and conflict between the two sides continued.

The Seljuk Turks were the first of several waves of Turkic people who would eventually establish themselves as the masters of the Byzantine Empire, granting to Asia Minor the name and the ruling race that it still has today. The origin of the Seljuks was as one of twenty-four Oğuz tribes of Central Asia, identifiable, like the Bulgars, as offshoots of the Huns of late antiquity. Tracing its ancestry to its founding warlord, Seljuk, an Oğuz warlord, by the tenth century the tribe had established itself on the Lower Jaxartes, a region overlapping the four corners of modern Uzbekistan, Tajikistan, Kyrgyzstan and Kazakhstan. Historical records reveal that the Byzantines first began taking note of their presence in Armenia in 1016. This raised considerable concern since Armenian loyalty was always suspect, and the kings of Armenia might just as easily throw their lot in with the Turks as sustain their loyalty to Constantinople. On the fringes of the Byzantine Empire, in the meanwhile, the Turks were indeed busy with their own empire-building, taking control of northern Persia during the 1040s under the Seljuk leader Tuğrul Bey. In 1055, Tuğrul marched on Baghdad and was welcomed by the Caliph as ruler and protector. In 1063 he died and was succeeded by his nephew Alp Arslan.

Alp Arslan, whose real name was Muhammad bin Daud Chaghri, was the second Sultan of the Seljuk Empire and great-grandson of Seljuk himself, and it is he who is credited with tipping the military balance against the Byzantines and commencing the Turkish settlement of Anatolia.

The name Alp Arslan (roughly translated from the Turkish to mean "Heroic Lion"), is one that resonates through Anatolian history with the same authority as Richard the Lionheart in Britain, or Vercingetorix in France. He was born in about 1029 (the precise date is disputed) in the Arab Empire's Persian province of Khurasan, serving initially under the command of his father, Daud Chaghri Beg, leader of Turkish forces in that region.[10] After the death of his father, Alp Arslan succeeded to the governorship of Khurasan, and later, in 1063, contested the succession after the death of Tuğrul. In this he prevailed by force of arms against his brother and his uncle in the Battle of Damghan in 1063. Thus he emerged as sultan of "Great Seljuk," sole ruler of an empire now stretching from the River Oxus, in modern Uzbekistan, to the River Tigris. The following year he directed his eye west, crossing the Euphrates, and after taking Caesarea Mazaca, the capital of Cappadocia, he moved against the Byzantine regions of Georgia and Armenia.[11]

---

[10] *Khurasan* or *Khorasan* was an historic region forming the northeast province of Greater Iran, congruent with eastern Iraq and western Iran on a modern map of the Middle East.

[11] *Cappadocia* was a historic region of Central Anatolia, largely encompassing the Nevşehir, Kayseri, Kırşehir, Aksaray and Niğde Provinces of

The various chronicles of Alp Arslan describe a military leader of uncommon resolve and ruthless brutality, whose use of mobile cavalry as the spearhead of his army proved devastatingly effective. His army first took on the Byzantines in three bruising campaigns, commencing in 1068, that ended in a comprehensive Turkish defeat and an inglorious return across the Euphrates. Alp Arslan, however, remained alert to any opportunity for a rematch, and that opportunity came in 1071 when the Byzantine Emperor Romanos IV Diogenes took to the field with a polyglot army of about 30,000 men to subdue Armenia. The two armies met at Manzikert, on the Murat River, north of Lake Van, where the epic Battle of Manzikert was fought.[12] This battle, well described in many historical texts, ended in a thorough rout of the Byzantines and the capture of their emperor.

This momentous moment in the history of Anatolia marked the beginning of the end of the Eastern Roman Empire, projecting the Seljuk Turks and the Sunni Muslims to predominance. While the Byzantine Empire would survive for almost four more centuries, and while the various crusades would challenge the matter, Manzikert marked the commencement of Turkish hegemony in Asia Minor.

The successors of Alp Arslan went on to expand and consolidate the empire until it encompassed most of Asia Minor, leaving just a strip along the Black Sea coast and pockets of the Aegean under Byzantine control. By 1078, the capital was established at Nicaea, and gradually the Seljuk empire became known as the Sultanate of Rum (the land of the Romans).

The Seljuk Empire was the penultimate Turkish empire, preceding the emergence of the Ottoman Empire. There is a school of historical thought that the erstwhile subjects of the Byzantine Empire welcomed the arrival of the Turks, but this could hardly have universally been the case. The arrival of Islam on the high plains of Anatolia and the east coast of the Mediterranean was accompanied by an enormous amount of trauma. Indeed, the frontline of such a radical religious transition could scarcely have been otherwise. Massacres, enslavements and forced conversions were a common feature of the first century of Turkish rule. The Christian Church came under transformational pressure, and it inevitably buckled, falling quickly thereafter into decline. However, despite the nomadic origins of the new imperial order, the empire was governed effectively and a settled state emerged from the transition fairly quickly. An interesting distribution of power saw provinces and regions governed by either appointed or hereditary emirs, with the unaffiliated or loosely affiliated tribal leaders remaining substantively led by their own beys and warlords.

Meanwhile, the comparatively swift conversion of Christian society to Muslim was not always achieved by coercion, for embracing Islam was often to gain access to the many benefits of Islam. Islam, for example, became the umbrella under which a great deal of scholarship was

---

Turkey.

[12] Lake Van, the largest lake in Anatolia, located in the far east of modern Turkey.

undertaken, in particular in medicine and law, the former of which was manifest by free hospitals, and the latter by courts of law that were extremely progressive in the context of the times. The thirteenth century marked the zenith of Seljuk civilization throughout Asia Minor, witnessing a flowering of artistic, administrative and military achievement, and a society of exaggerated civilization and devotion to enlightened principles.

The Seljuks left a substantial material legacy throughout Turkey, and traces of the distinctive Seljuk architectural style can be found as far afield as Pakistan. That style, as historians have often observed, borrowed much from a tradition of tents, being often octagonal or decagonal, and typically adorned with elaborate decoration featuring distinctive motifs of swirls and loops and fine tilework and mosaic. Tiles of glazed faience frequently lined the interior walls, which were typically supported by tent-like posts. This was a precursor to the development of the brilliant blue and white tiles that, over the course of the next few centuries, would come to define the finesse and accomplishment of Turkish architecture.

Besides the enormous changes wrought in culture and religion by the rise of the Turks, there came a liberalization of the economy and a gradual relaxation on the strictures of society. The wider economy remained premised on agriculture, but increased market opportunities and improvements in transport uplifted agricultural production from simple subsistence to more market-oriented production. Perhaps the most important stimulus for economic growth, however, was the development and protection of roads and other transport infrastructure, and the establishment of widely dispersed markets for the sale and exchange of produce. Cities and ports, on the whole, in particular those most associated with the main international trade routes, flourished in an environment of tolerance and open trade. The fourteenth century traveler and historian Ibn Battuta remarked on the division of cities like Antalya, today the second most populous city in Turkey and a major Aegean port, into separate cantons for Muslims, Jews and Christians, and the open welcome extended to travelers and merchants of all nationalities.

As a result, the arrival of the Seljuks marked a profound sea-change in the culture of Asia Minor. While many Greeks fled west in the aftermath of these upheavals, many others remained to be absorbed into Turkish society, becoming Turkish speakers, until, by the fifteenth century, the entity of Asia Minor was Turkish speaking.

In 1095, the Byzantine Emperor Alexios I Komnenos submitted a request to Pope Urban II for a force of knights to assist in the ongoing Byzantine struggle against the Turks, in particular, the Seljuks. The cause of liberating the Christian sites did not necessarily move the Byzantines, but any assistance in the reestablishment of Byzantine control of Asia minor would be welcomed. While the Crusaders did indeed roll back the Turks, and by extension return territory to the Byzantines, the region also suffered much from the heavy hand of the Crusader advance, and even more so from the propensity of individual knights to install themselves in minor kingdoms. Bohemond the Norman, for example, leader of the first crusade, named himself prince of

Antioch, while Baldwin of Boulogne became count of Edessa and first king of Jerusalem. Although owing nominal fealty to the Byzantine Empire, the Crusaders deported themselves very much as a power unto themselves.

In 114, the Second Crusade began its disorderly march south through Asia Minor, wreaking significant devastation in its path. This time the relationship between the Crusaders and the Byzantines was extremely tense, which had much to do with the fact that this crusade was led directly by two European kings, namely Louis VII of France and Conrad III of Germany, assisted by a number of other prominent European nobles. Among the latter was Frederick Barbarossa, the future Holy Roman Emperor Frederick I. It was he who encouraged and aided the Seljuk leader Kilik Arslan I to take on the Byzantines, which, in short, resulted in the epic Byzantine defeat at the Battle of Myriokephalon in 1176. This devasting reverse effectively ended the Byzantine quest to recover the interior of Anatolia from the grip of the Turks. It also weakened the empire to the extent that the various Balkan provinces detached themselves, never to return.

In 1187, Frederick Barbarossa led the Third Crusade, but this effort did not have quite the same impact after Frederick died near Silifke Castle in southern Anatolia, drowned while crossing the Saleph River. The Fourth Crusade assembled in Venice in 1201 with the implicit understanding that it would take the Byzantine imperial capital of Constantinople before moving on to the Holy Land. Thus, two years later Constantinople was under siege and on 13 April 1204 the walls were breached. Sir Steven Runciman, author of the definitive A History of the Crusades, made this observation:

There have been few crimes against humanity that match the Fourth Crusade. Not only did it cause the destruction or dispersal of all of the treasures of the past that Byzantium had devotedly stored, and the mortal wounding of a civilization that was still active and great, but it was also an act of gigantic political folly. It brought no help to the Christians in Palestine. Instead, it robbed them of political helpers, and it upset the whole defense of Christendom. [13] Indeed, the Crusaders abandoned the idea of marching on the Holy Land altogether, settling instead on crowning Count Baldwin of Flanders the first Latin Emperor of Constantinople. For all intents and purposes, the Empire of Byzantium ceased to exist.

These events coincided with the commencement of a slow decline of the Seljuk state which came about primarily because of the arrival on the scene of the Mongols under the successors of Genghis Khan. In 1241, the Mongols took Erzurum in eastern Anatolia, and in 1242 the Seljuks suffered a major defeat at Kuzdagan, today a village in the extreme northwest of Iran. Sporadic uprisings in the east resulted in the sacking of numerous Seljuk cities, while the Mamelukes of Egypt seized the opportunity presented by the confusion to overthrow the Crusader kingdoms. From this gathering imbroglio, however, emerged the Ottoman Turks, who by the 1420s had

---

[13] Runciman, Steven. *A History of the Crusades Volume III*. (Cambridge University Press, Cambridge, 1951) p130

stripped the Empire of Constantinople of all of its territories besides the city itself.

During the twelfth and thirteenth centuries, as the Seljuk Turks established their empire and the settled state surrounding it, nomadic Turkoman tribes proliferated in a series of emirates on its borders. These itinerant warrior bands were known as gazis, and they styled themselves soldiers of Islam. One such dynasty in northern Phrygia was founded by a Turkic warlord by the name of Osman Gazi. According to subsequent Ottoman tradition, Osman descended from the Kayi tribe of the Oghuz Turks, arriving in north-central Anatolia as part of the general westward movement of the Turkomans. His tribe was known as the "Osmanlis," only later adapted by Europeans as "Ottomans." In 1326, Osman captured the city of Prusa, now the modern Turkish city of Bursa, situated more or less on the opposite shore of the Sean of Marmara from Constantinople. This site was established as the Ottoman capital, and against a backdrop of waning Mongol influence in the east and the steady decline of the Seljuks, Osman was able to create a counterbalancing stable state in Anatolia.

Osman I died in 1224 and was succeeded by Orhan Gazi, a dynamic military leader who swiftly added to the Ottoman realm the major cities of Nicaea, Nicomedia, Scutari and Karesi, which implies both the east shore of the Sea of Marmara and the south shore of the Black Sea immediately north of Constantinople. He also established a base of operation on the Gallipoli Peninsula from where he began conducting raids both into Thrace and against the Serbian Empire of Stefan Uroš IV Dušan. Added to these military adventures he went on the diplomatic offensive, marrying his daughter to the Byzantine emperor John VI.

Orhan was succeeded by Murat I, who served as Ottoman Sultan from 1362-1389. Murat added Thrace, Macedonia, Bulgaria and Serbia to the expanding Ottoman territories. At the end of Murat's reign, then, it could reasonably be said that the Ottoman Empire was established. To a great extent, the Turks did not interfere much with the established systems of Byzantine rule, retaining preexisting administrative systems and borrowing much in terms of cultural substance from the Byzantines, and intermarriage between established familial ties between the two kingdoms.

The Ottomans were supported by a well-constructed military system put in place by Orhan which was to endure for centuries. He adopted and adapted the Seljuk system of gathering Christian youth to be brought up as military slaves, owing first and absolute loyalty to the Sultan, which acted as a useful counterweight to the power of the great nobles. These were the household troops, a kind of Praetorian Guard known as the Kapıkulu, or the "Slaves of the Porte."[14] To this was added a strong infantry element to the sipâhi, or the traditional cavalry of the Turks, named the yeñiçeri and later Westernized as the "Janissary."

This steady and ordered Ottoman expansion was abruptly and briefly interrupted by the

---

[14] The *Sublime Porte* was the term for the central government of the Ottoman Empire.

explosive irruption of the Tartars under the leadership of Timur, better known in the West as Tamerlane. In 1402, the armies of the Ottomans and the Tartars met near Ankara where the Ottomans were defeated. A year later, however, Tamerlane died of illness during a winter campaign causing the vigor of the Tartar incursion to dissipate. The Ottoman Empire was then reunited under Mehmet I (1413–1421) and his successor Murat II (1421–1451).

Throughout all of this, the city of Constantinople remained undisturbed, but inevitably it resided within the field of vision of successive Ottoman sultans as the ultimate prize of empire. Between 1444 and 1481, with a brief interruption, the empire was ruled by Mehmet II, known also as Mehmet the Conqueror, and it was he who defined as an objective the capture of Constantinople. His goal was to establish himself as the leader of Islam, creating a world empire and halting once and for all the debilitating effect of the Crusades. It is also interesting that upon his succession, Mehmet ordered the killing of all of his brothers to eliminate any possible rivals, which established something of a tradition that would be followed upon the succession of any new sultan. On the European side of the Bosporus, Mehmet built a strong fortress, setting the stage for an assault on Constantinople. Needless to say, the emperor and citizens of Constantinople watched this development with alarm. Past sieges had always been thwarted by the hitherto impregnable city wall, but this time there was a sense that things would be different.

The siege of Constantinople began in February 1453. A defending force of some 7,000 peered over the parapets at a besieging army of 60,000, supported by a weapon never before deployed against the walls of Constantinople – artillery. Brought on to the battlefield was a Hungarian cannon, the largest ever built, and when it commenced fire against the city walls, it became clear that the end would not be long in coming. The damage caused by this barrage of cannon fire is still visible on the ruins of the city walls today. On May 29, those walls were finally breached at a point near the gate of Saint Romanos through which the Turks poured in.

The fall of Constantinople effectively marked the end of the Byzantine Empire which had existed officially since 395, enduring for more than a thousand years. A minor enclave of the empire survived for a few years as the Empire of Trebizond, or the Trapezuntine Empire. Territorially limited to pockets along the southeast shore of the Black sea, the empire, echoing the old city-states, focused on the city of that name. Of all the Byzantine successor states, Trebizon would survive the longest, but in the 1450s it came under Ottoman attack, and in 1461, after a month-long siege, the city fell.

The Ottoman Empire

With the fall of Constantinople, Anatolia was, for the first time, dominated wholly and completely by the Turks. While Turkey was no more than a constituent territory of a much larger empire that encompassed, at its greatest extent, land from the Balkans to Egypt, the heartland of the empire became known to the Western powers as "Turkey."

However, in broad brushstrokes, Mehmet's first task upon his conquest of Constantinople was to commence the regeneration of a city that had settled into a long era of decay. Roads, aqueducts and sewers were rebuilt, a souk was constructed to facilitate a renewal of trade, and the glory of the new ruler was embodied in the Topkapi Palace, today one of the great architectural treasures of the Turkish cultural capital. The great Mosque of Fatih Mehmet was built to celebrate the new predominance of Islam, and a diminishing population was boosted by the importation of thousands of Muslims. Of the 100,000 or so citizens of Constantinople in the aftermath of its conquest, more than half were Muslim, while the remainder were mostly Greeks, Armenians and Jews. Constantinople, however, did not become the capital of the Ottoman Empire until the reign of Selim I in 1512.

An interesting aspect of Ottoman administration was established when Mehmet appointed a new patriarch, Gennadius Scholarius, whom he elevated to both the civil and religious leadership of the Greeks. This established the Millet, or a system of autonomous government by which each ethnic group, nation and community within the Ottoman Empire was ruled by its own authorities under the overall rule of the sultan. This did not mean independence, but simply a system of indirect rule.

Mehmet also applied a great deal energy and pragmatism to the regeneration of trade. Industries were established, most notably textiles, but more importantly, trade relations with the West were forged, in particular with the important trade centers of Venice and Genoa. This established Constantinople as a major trade center and allowed for the entry and circulation of both Europeans and European ideas. In the meanwhile, the wars of conquest continued, adding to the empire in increments the Balkans, Albania, Greece, Crimea and the Island of Rhodes. These wars continued under the successors of Mehmet, and it is perhaps worth noting that, under Selim I, who ruled from 1512-1520, shipyards were constructed on the Golden Horn and for the first time, the Ottoman Empire emerged as a significant naval power. The rise of the Ottoman Empire was characterized by enormous cultural advances which reached their apogee under the rule of Suleiman I, better known as Suleiman the Magnificent, who reigned from 1520-1566.

Suleiman came to the throne unopposed thanks to the custom of killing all potential rivals. His father, Selim I, put to death all of his four brothers, his nephews and all of his sons with the exception of Suleiman. By the era of Suleiman, Constantinople was a well-established destination for European diplomats, and the court of the Sultan and the city of Constantinople itself was famous for its opulence and splendor. A first-hand account of this can be found in the letters of Ogier Ghiselin de Busbecq, the envoy of Charles V, the Holy Roman Emperor: "Now come with me and cast your eye over the immense crowd of turbaned heads, wrapped in countless folds of whitest silk and bright raiment of every kind and hue, and everywhere the brilliance of gold, silver, purple, silk and satin."

Concurrent with the emergence of this artistic and cultural Golden Age, the wars of conquest and acquisition continued. The rise of the Hapsburg Empire presented the Ottomans for the first time with an opponent of comparable size and influence. The conquest of Belgrade and Rhodes, however, gave the empire a foothold in Europe from which to mount further advances. Ottoman naval activity dominated the Aegean while the economic authority of the Empire impacted heavily the trade dominance of Venice, which, in 1540, was forced to concede its interests in Greece to the Turks.

On the other side, the opulence of Suleiman's rule and the ongoing expansion placed a massive financial burden on the Empire, and as the population increased with wider conquest, and the tax burden grew ever heavier, the rule of the Janissaries became an ever more characteristic feature of the empire. As regional uprisings became a regular occurrence, the empire inherited by Selim II was one increasingly divided. The rise in importance and power of the Grand Vizier, an administrative role not dissimilar to a prime minister, often overshadowed the authority of the sultan, and indeed, after Suleiman, no sultan of his caliber, or that of Mehmet's, would emerge. By the mid-seventeenth century, the Janissary corps had swelled to some 200,000 men, and with the relaxation of many of its founding conventions, it became corrupt, carving out virtual private fiefdoms in the outlying regions. Most drew wages and titles but took no part in military campaigns, and the dead weight of their existence and their reactionary nature tended to support the decline and inertia of Turkish rule.

Suleiman the Magnificent

In January 1699, the Great Turkish War, or the War of the Holy League, was concluded with the signing of the Treaty of Karlowitz. This sixteen-year war was fought between the Ottoman Empire and the Holy League, which consisted of the Habsburg Monarchy, Poland-Lithuania, Venice and Russia. The war ended in the defeat of the Ottoman Empire and the loss of a significant amount of territory, including Hungary and the Polish–Lithuanian Commonwealth as well as part of the western Balkans. This left the Ottoman Empire for the first time to deal with its European neighbors and rivals from a position of weakness. Turkey now became known as the "Poor Man of Europe," and as the eighteenth century progressed, to the emerging powers of Europe – France, Austria, Britain and Russia – the Ottoman Empire became a candidate ripe for dismemberment.

In 1770, on the back of numerous Russian fomented revolts in the Balkans and the Peloponnese, the Russian and Turkish fleets met at Çeşme on the Aegean coast, and there, a spectacular Ottoman defeat opened up the Mediterranean to the Russians. A year later Russia occupied Crimea. Then came the French Revolution and the rise of Napoleon Bonaparte, which presented a sudden threat to the Ottoman Empire from a hitherto friendly France. Napoleon's expedition to Egypt rattled the outer dominions of the empire, and although short-lived, it set in motion the eventual loss of that important territory. The final loss of the land came in 1838 when Mehmet Ali declared de facto independence and defeated an Ottoman attempt to regain it.

And thus, the trend continued. In 1830, after a bloody revolt, Greece extracted herself from Ottoman control. The Crimean War was fought between 1853 and 1856, pitting the Russian Empire against a coalition of the Ottoman Empire, Britain, France and Sardinia, in which the latter won, but in doing so the Ottoman were compromised towards Britain and France.

There was a certain amount of strategic advantage in maintaining the weak and corrupt Ottomans as a buffer against the Russians, but to a large extent the empire had lost control over its own destiny. The 1878 Congress of Berlin declared the independence of Romania, Serbia and Bulgaria, and during the Balkan Wars of 1912 and 1913, almost the entirety of Ottoman Europe was lost.

Then, as the dark clouds of war began to gather over Europe, the Ottoman Empire made the fateful decision to ally itself with Germany, Austria-Hungary and Bulgaria in the "Quadruple Alliance." As a consequence, in 1914, Turkey went to war as an ally of the Central Powers of Europe.

An Independent Turkey

In the same way that France sought the support of the Sublime Porte in its fight against central European powers during the 16th century, Germany saw the Ottoman Empire as a possible strategic partner against Russia, France, and England. German Kaiser Wilhelm II visited the Ottoman Empire on two occasions before World War I and sought to encourage Abdul Hamid's pan-Islamism, which he saw as a useful tool against the British colonialism. During his second visit in 1898, the Kaiser visited the tomb of Saladin in Damascus and offered to pay for its renovation. Arab newspapers praised the visit, stating that the Kaiser was "the best friend of the great Sultan;" and "the most sincere and loyal monarch in his friendship toward the Sultan." The German Emperor even earned the title of "Hajji Wilhelm."

Wilhelm II

Economic relations expanded with the building of the Baghdad Railway, starting in 1903. The Prussian and later German military expertise was also increasingly used by the Ottoman army, peaking with the German mission of 1913, led by German military officer Otto Liman von Sanders.

Despite that, the Ottoman Empire did not initially seek to formally ally with Germany, much less participate in a global conflict. In fact, as the 1910s dawned, the growing rivalry between the Entente alliance (France, Russia, and Britain)[15] and the Central Powers (the Austro-Hungarian Empire and Germany), seemed like a distant problem. Ironically, the Ottoman Empire sought on multiple occasions to enter into an alliance with the British, French and Russians, or to at least

---

[15] Referring to the Triple Entente, an agreement between these three powers signed in the wake of the "Entente Cordiale" (Cordial Friendship) treaty between France and England in 1904 and the Anglo-Russian Entente of 1907.

secure an agreement regarding its neutrality during a potential conflict. The alliance with Russia was, however, more central to the British and French, who refused the various Ottoman proposals.

The disastrous war against the Balkan states brought together the changes needed to convince the Ottomans of the benefit of the alliance with the Kaiser. Things would go entirely south from there, with the brief exception of the Ottoman victory in the Gallipoli campaign.

While the Gallipoli Campaign had been a major defeat for the Allies, there were no real winners. Both sides had lost about a quarter of a million men in dead, wounded, or seriously ill. At its height, half of the Ottoman army had been stationed in the Dardanelles, greatly weakening its efforts on all other fronts, draining an already overtaxed war effort of men, munitions, and supplies. Turkey remembers Gallipoli as one great victory in an otherwise disastrous war. Just as importantly, it helped establish Mustafa Kemal as a hero.

Mustafa Kemal during the war

On July 3, 1918, Sultan Mehmed V died, ceding the throne to Mehmed VI, the 36th and final Sultan of the Ottoman Empire. Mustafa Kemal was recalled to the capital and reassigned to the Seventh Army in Palestine, where they had to deal with the Arab Revolt, a concentrated British effort to dismember the Ottoman Empire's grip on Arabia and the Levant by supporting the nationalist aspirations of the Arabs, led by the Hashemite Sharif and Emir of Mecca. This was the theater of operations for Lawrence of Arabia, the British soldier and diplomat who facilitated and participated in the revolt. The Sharifian forces, led by Hussein, and with significant British support, successfully drove Ottoman forces from most of Transjordan and the Hejaz, taking Damascus on October 1, 1918.

Mustafa Kemal assumed his command in Palestine as these events were playing out. He briefly attended his headquarters in Nablus towards the end of August 1918 as the Seventh Army strained to hold the central sector of the long and disintegrating line. From September 19-25, the final Allied breakthrough was achieved at the Battle of Megiddo, known to the Turks as the the Rout of Nablus. The Turkish Eighth Army, holding the coastal flank, collapsed, and Mustafa Kemal was ordered by General von Sanders, the German commander of Turkish forces in Palestine, to fall back to the north to avoid envelopment by advancing Allied forces. The Seventh Army fought a spirited rearguard action, and although it was badly damaged by British attacks, a defensive line north of Aleppo was held.

In the meanwhile, negotiations for an armistice were underway on board the HMS *Agamemnon*, anchored in Moudros harbor on the Greek island of Lemnos. On October 30, 1918, the Armistice of Mudros was signed. This required the Ottomans to surrender all their remaining garrisons outside of Anatolia and the forts securing the entrance to the Dardanelles, the location of the most bruising Allied encounter with the Turks. Immediately after the signing, Mustafa Kemal was appointed to the command of the Yildirim Army Group, taking over from Pasha Liman, a command that he held until the formation's disbandment a few days later. By mid-November, he was back in the Ottoman capital, now in accordance with the terms of the Armistice of Mudros, and alongside the second city of İzmir, occupied by British, French, and Italian forces. Although this marked the practical end of the Ottoman Empire, the edifice would remain standing for a few years yet. It was also the moment, as most historians tend to agree, that Mustafa Kemal transitioned from a military commander to a revolutionary leader.

On April 30, 1919, Mustafa Kemal, with the effective rank of major-general, was appointed to the Ninth Army Inspectorate and given the task of reorganizing what remained of Ottoman forces scattered across Anatolia. He was also ordered to "improve internal security," which he realized could carry many implications, and to carry out the task, he was ordered to establish his headquarters in the city of Samsun, on Turkey's Black Sea coast, about 500 miles distant from Constantinople. He had been one of the Ottoman Empire's most successful military officers during World War I, but by then, his allegiance had passed entirely to the revolutionary movement, still nascent and unformed, and while he retained his commission for a while, he did so under increasingly stern orders from the capital to cease his independent activity and return to Constantinople. He politely refused both commands as he began to position himself more forcefully in the leadership of a nationalist movement.

Mustafa Kemal was still only 38, but he owned the stature of senior rank and the seasoned air of a mature commander. He also possessed an intangible extra dimension of leadership that many in the senior command were beginning to acknowledge and respect. He was a patriot, but he was also supremely ambitious, and he recognized that the moment was now. World War I had been instructive, for it forged within him an intuitive understanding of the race of people upon which this burden of revolution now rested. Patrick Kinross explained, "Kemal saw the Turkish people without illusion. He knew that they were dour, conservative, fatalistic, slow in mind and initiative. But he knew also that they were stubborn, patient, capable of endurance; a race of fighters ruthless in battle, responsive to leadership and ready to die to order."[16]

The occupation of Constantinople and Smyrna provided the perfect and obvious vehicle upon which to build a head of revolutionary steam, and he issued instructions to all the civil and military authorities within his region to maintain a steady barrage of complaints to the Ottoman capital about it. The British, as the senior Allied partner, wished to tread very carefully at this uncertain juncture, and as the Paris Peace Conference recast the map of Europe, Africa, and Asia Minor, the steady drumbeat of nationalist opposition emanating from Samsun and the wider Anatolian countryside was an embarrassment to both the British and Ottoman officials there. At the same time, Mustafa Kemal set about reorganizing all the surviving Turkish army units in Anatolia and Thrace, positioning them as a potential army of revolution.

As he pressured the Allies, the Allies pressured the Ottomans, until the angry demands that he immediately return to Constantinople were replaced by hapless requests that he also politely ignored. He moved his headquarters inland to the village of Havza, and there the first active cell of the resistance was established. Quickly the mood spread across Smyrna as military officers led their detachments across to join the brewing revolution. Loyal Turkish forces attempted to damp the movement down, but they could not be relied upon, and so they were soon withdrawn. Kemal then moved still further east to the city of Amasya.

Meanwhile, as the Paris Conference droned on, President Woodrow Wilson, taking into account current European politics, announced that he was contemplating an American mandate over Armenia, Constantinople, and the Straits. This, in many respects, was a godsend for Mustafa Kemal, as it offered yet more ammunition to fire the nationalist passions of his people. The mandate principle was a solution provided by the League of Nations to the problem of governing German and Turkish imperial territories that were liberated during the war and left without government. Few had any recent traditions or institutions of independent leadership, and so it was believed necessary to allocate governing mandates to the victorious powers to provide

---

[16] Kinross, Patrick. *Ataturk*. Orion Publishing Group. Kindle Edition.

some degree of interim management. This was not the case for Turkey proper, which was very well-governed indeed, but what the future might hold for the the crumbling empire of the Ottomans was very much on the minds of the convening powers. Needless to say, even the tentative suggestion of a great power mandate over any part of Turkey provoked a barrage of protests from Mustafa Kemal and his gathering movement.

In Amasya, a picturesque hill town in northern Anatolia, a revolutionary manifesto known as the "Amasya Circular" was drafted and distributed. The signatories of the document were Mustafa Kemal and three other senior officers: Fahri Yaver-i Hazret-i Şehriyari, Rauf Orbay, Miralay Refet Bele and Mirliva (Major-General) Ali Fuat Cebesoy. It is generally agreed among historians that this document was the first written notification of the commencement of the Turkish War of Independence. Stripped of its slogans and declarations, the document simply stated that Turkey's independence, indeed, its very existence, was under threat. To devise a strategy to meet this threat, a national conference was to be held in Sivas, a city in north-central Anatolia, prior to which a preparatory conference was to be held in July 1919 at the city of Erzurum in eastern Anatolia. In preparation, Kemal took the risky decision to resign his commission, uncertain when he did whether his senior commanders would continue to recognize his leadership.[17] They did, and approaching the coming struggle with his political rather than his military persona at the fore appeared only to strengthen his position.

The doors of the Erzurum Congress opened on July 23, 1919, admitting 56 delegates, and it continued in session until August 4. One of the first orders of business was to elect Mustafa Kemal chairman of the Congress, after which several key resolutions were passed. One of the most important was to leave open the possibility of forming a national government independent of Constantinople. Remaining ostensibly loyal to the Ottoman Empire, the Congress also affirmed a popular rejection of partition and a universal desire to remain within the empire. It was added that no special provisions would be made for Christian Greeks and Armenians. Then, a representative committee was elected with Mustafa Kemal at its head. Not surprisingly, these events provoked another bout of desperate histrionics from Constantinople, but the severity of the official response never rose much above that.

From Havza and Amasya, by organizing and realigning the military forces of Anatolia, Mustafa Kemal had effectively launched a military resistance, at the head of which he placed himself. At Erzurum, he launched a parallel political movement, of which he again assumed the inevitable leadership role. This placed him in a dominant position to approach the now iconic Sivas Congress.

The Congress at Sivas was held from September 4-11, 1919 as events were beginning to accelerate towards some sort of dénouement. The Ottoman Empire was for all intents and purposes defunct, and it and many of the major provincial cities were under Allied occupation.

---

[17] In fact, his dismissal from the armed forces was probably by then imminent.

The occupation, however, was at a garrison level, and it certainly could not be said that the occupying powers had any real control over the country. The situation was in flux, and Mustafa Kemal was the one most likely to succeed.

The delegate count at Sivas was smaller than Erzurum, but it represented a wider geographic spread. The proceedings of the conference were arcane and rather convoluted, but in essence they amounted to a challenge to the imperial government, which meant, in practical terms, a challenge to the Allies. An alliance of Turkish resistance organizations was confirmed under a pact known as *Misak-ı Millî*, (the National Pact). Fresh elections were called for, after which it was understood that the Ottoman Chamber of Deputies would be required to consider the conclusions and proposals of the Sivas Congress. As expected, the Allied response to this was to dissolve the Chamber, which undermined the last pillar upon which the edifice stood, reducing the empire to a few symbolic vestiges dutifully hostile to the Turkish National Movement.

Mustafa Kemal and others at the Sivas Congress

An election was held in December 1919, and Mustafa Kemal was by then established in the city of Ankara in central Anatolia, making no secret of his intention to guide the movement towards a republic. An overwhelming majority was returned in favor of candidates representing the "Association for Defense of Rights for Anatolia and Roumelia" (*Anadolu ve Rumeli Müdafaa-i Hukuk Cemiyet*), controlled by Mustafa Kemal himself.[18] There was belligerent posturing on the part of the Allied occupiers, but Mustafa Kemal was reasonably safe in his

---

[18] *Roumelia*, of course, was the old 'Land of the Romans,' comprising modern Bulgaria, Greece, Albania and North Macedonia.

belief that no costly or risky military expeditions were likely to overturn or frustrate these advances. The serving Grand Vizier, Damat Ferid Pasha, pleaded with the Allies for military support against the rebels, but this was not granted. Instead, the British withdrew their garrisons from regions of Anatolia identified as irredeemable, leaving the western rim of Anatolia securely in nationalist rebel hands. Damat Ferid Pasha was removed, and as an indication of the way things were going, the political voice of Mustafa Kemal began to be heard for the first time in the national press and the activities of the nationalist movement were now widely reported. Within a span of a little over four months since his arrival in Samsun, Mustafa Kemal had engineered the collapse of the government and brought down the pro-Allied Grand Vizier. Just as importantly, he had sent a powerful message to the Allies that they were no longer dealing with a compliant and supplicating imperial remnant, but a powerful and growing nationalist movement that had ideas of its own with regards to Turkey's future.

The fourth and final term of the Ottoman parliament opened on January 12, 1920, sitting in Constantinople until March 18, when it was dissolved by the occupying British administration, who adopted soon afterwards the National Pact. This, by way of recapitulation, comprised six decisions made by this final parliament. Parliament met in session on January 28, a fortnight after its opening, and the decisions reached were announced on February 12. The decisions were taken against a backdrop of a caucus of parliamentarians loyal to Mustafa Kemal and calling themselves *Felâh-ı Vatan*. The group was established to confirm the decisions taken at both the Erzurum and Sivas Congresses, and as Mustafa Kemal himself observed, "It is the nation's iron fist that writes the Nation's Oath which is the main principle of our independence to the annals of history."[19]

The essential tenets of the National Pact were as follows:

- The future of the territories inhabited by an Arab majority at the time of the signing of the Armistice of Mudros will be determined by a referendum. On the other hand, the territories which were not occupied at that time and were inhabited by a Turkish majority are the homeland of the Turkish nation.
- The status of Kars, Ardahan and Batum may be determined by a referendum.
- The status of Western Thrace will be determined by the votes of its inhabitants.
- The security of Constantinople and Marmara should be provided for. Transport and free trade on the Straits of the Bosporus and the Dardanelles will be determined by Turkey and other concerned countries.
- The rights of minorities will be issued on condition that the rights of the Muslim minorities in neighboring countries are protected.
- In order to develop in every field, the country should be independent and free; all restrictions on political, judicial and financial development will be removed.[20]

---

[19] Butler, Daniel, Allen. *Shadow of the Sultan's Realm: The Destruction of the Ottoman Empire and the Creation of the Modern Middle East.* (Potomac Books, Washington DC) p119

It is difficult not to regard this series of provision as a direct challenge to the Allies, and particularly the British. Mustafa Kemal issued a call for an election for a new national assembly that would sit in Ankara, to be known as the Grand National Assembly. This assembly, he said, would possess extraordinary powers, and upon its benches past members of the Chamber of Deputies would be allowed to sit for the sake of as wide a representation as possible.

The election was held as proposed, following the same electoral procedures as previously applied to the Chamber of Deputies, and thus were elected the first sitting members of the new Grand National Assembly. The Grand National Assembly held its inaugural session on April 23, 1920.

Matters came to a head on August 10, 1920, when Damat Ferid Pasha, reinstated as Grand Vizier, signed on behalf of the Sultan the Treaty of Sèvres, which finalized the plan to partition the Ottoman Empire. This treaty was just one of many signed by the members of the Central Powers in the aftermath of the war, and in the case of the signed Treaty of Sèvres, it cleared the way for the British to govern Palestine and Iraq as mandates, while the French would govern Syria and Lebanon by mandate. Besides numerous financial and military limitations and restrictions, the terms of the treaty created new territorial zones of influence over and above the French and British mandates, favoring Greece, France, and Italy. Armenia was recognized as an established state, while various other provisions were included to govern navigation through the Bosporus and the Dardanelles. Several free zones were created, Thrace was yielded to the Greeks, and Kurdistan was granted the right to decide its future by referendum.

In response to this, Kemal demanded absolute and complete independence and a guarantee of the safeguarding of Turkish interests on Turkish soil. Thus, the gauntlet was thrown down, and all sides prepared for war.

The Turkish War of Independence was a complex and multifaceted affair, and Mustafa Kemal led and pushed the Grand National Assembly to authorize the formation of a National Army to be drawn from the disparate elements of the rebellious Ottoman detachments. The Army of the Grand National Assembly then faced the vastly weakened army of the Caliphate, heavily buttressed by Allied forces. The initial confrontations took place on two fronts, in the east against the Armenians (backed by the French) and in the west against the Greeks, who had occupied Smyrna, Cyprus, and the Aegean Islands in the spring of 1919. In both instances, forces under Mustafa Kemal's command were victorious, largely thanks to solid leadership and copious material and military support provided by the Soviets. An unfortunate corollary of Turkish successes against the Armenians was the orchestrated massacre of up to 12,000 Armenians, which undercut the Armenian population in Turkish Anatolia to a remnant.

In August 1921, Mustafa Kamel was appointed Commander-in-Chief of the force of the Grand

National Assembly, which made him arguably the most powerful man on either side of the field. Now using the informal title of *Atatürk* ("Father of Turkey"), he took on the Greeks at the Battle of Sakarya. This was a sprawling and grueling three-week campaign fought alongside the banks of the Sakarya River, which empties into the south shore of the Black Sea. It ended in a narrow Turkish victory, and in the opinions of most historians, it marked the most important turning point in the Turkish War of Independence. According to Turkish historian, writer, and literary critic İsmail Habip Sevük, "[T]he retreat that started in Vienna on 13 September 1683 stopped 238 years later."[21]

While the Battle of Sakarya ended conclusively any Greek hopes of imposing a settlement on Turkey by force of arms, resulting instead in a graceless retreat, Atatürk returned to Ankara in triumph, where he was rewarded by promotion to the rank of Mareşal (Field Marshall) and given the additional traditional title of Gazi.[22] These victories spurred Atatürk and his army on to even greater endeavors, and when the Allies sought a reduced and modified peace settlement based on a watered-down version of the Treaty of Sèvres, the Turks refused and launched a comprehensive assault on the crumbling Greek lines. In August 1922, the Battle of Dumlupınar, the last battle of the Turkish War of Independence, was fought. The fighting took place near Dumlupınar, a small town in the Aegean region of Turkey, and resulted in yet another Greek defeat and the reclamation of the whole of Smyrna by Turkish forces on September 9, 1922.

The results of the Battle of Dumlupınar finally brought it home to the Allies that the severe terms of the Treaty of Sèvres simply would not prevail, and to end the war a renegotiation was required. A conference was held in the Swiss city of Lausanne between November 1922 and July 1923 involving delegates from Britain, France, Italy, and Turkey. Turkey was represented by General İsmet İnönü, Rıza Nur, better known as İsmet Pasha, and Chief Rabbi Chaim Nahum. The conference was coordinated and dominated by the British Foreign Secretary Lord Curzon.

---

[21] Fleet, Kate. *Suraiya Faroqhi, Reşat Kasaba: The Cambridge History of Turkey* Volume 4 (Cambridge University Press, Cambridge, 2008) p138.

[22] According to Wikipedia: *Ghazi* – '[O]riginally referred to individuals who participated in *ghazw*, meaning military expeditions or raiding. The latter term was applied in early Islamic literature to expeditions led by the Islamic prophet Muhammad, and later taken up by Turkic military leaders to describe their wars of conquest.

Atatürk at the Battle of Dumlupınar

For 11 weeks the two sides negotiated, and proceedings were enlivened considerably by the sparring and gamesmanship of both Lord Curzon and İsmet Pasha. Lord Curzon, in the twilight of a long and august domestic and foreign service career, including as Viceroy of India, had a tendency to be hectoring and bullying, while the latter, considerably younger, was subtly humorous and deceptively self-deprecating. As the story goes, when Curzon settled into his customary harangues, deriding Turkey's position and thumping the table over Allied demands, İsmet Pasha, who was almost entirely deaf, removed his hearing aid and read quietly until his counterpart exhausted himself, after which he returned his hearing aid and continued to press his own demands.

The net result of it all, after plenty of acrimony and adjournments, was a treaty signed on July 24, 1923 known as the Treaty of Lausanne. The Treaty of Lausanne provided for the independence of Turkey with built-in protections for Greek Orthodox Christian minorities in Turkey and Muslim minorities in Greece. These populations, however, in particular the Greek Christians of Turkey, had by then been diminished by expulsions and purges, so aside from small pockets in Constantinople, the issue was largely academic. The question of Turkish Armenians had also been largely resolved by the phases of the Armenian Genocide that commenced more or less at the onset of World War I and continued almost to the date of the signing of the Treaty of Lausanne. Various territorial adjustments were agreed to, especially as they affected Greek interests, Cyprus, British-administered Egypt, and Anglo-Egyptian Sudan. Turkey conceded the loss to Cyprus and renounced all claim to the Dodecanese Islands.

On October 29, 1923, the Republic of Turkey was proclaimed, and the Ottoman Empire formally came to an end.

Atatürk on the cover of *Time* in 1923

Atatürk in 1924

When the Treaty of Lausanne was signed at the Palais de Rumine in the Swiss city of Lausanne, one of the signatories of the document was Atatürk himself, and by dint of his revolutionary credentials and leadership of the Grand National Assembly, he took his place as the first President of an independent Turkey, formally taking office on October 29, 1923. It was not until 1934 that the honorific "Atatürk" was formally given to him, but by then the name had been his for a long time. As Mustafa Kemal Atatürk, he would rule the nation as an icon until his death in 1938.

Atatürk, who was only 43 when he took office, was faced with two immediate challenges. The first was to establish a condition of complete national independence, and by this he meant not only political, financial, military, and judicial independence, but also cultural independence. In this sense, it's important to keep in mind his thoughts at a younger age on the contrasts between Arab religious administration and Western-style secular government. Cultural and political independence need not, in his mind, preclude borrowing ideas from outside systems of government that were proven to work. Indeed, a dedicated branch of government was created to study the constitutions, legal codes, and systems of administration of the leading Western powers.

From these, an authentically Turkish system of secular democracy was devised and came into effect. Much of this was driven personally by Atatürk, and as most historians would agree, his signature achievement was to recreate the Turkish people's self-image. Instead of viewing themselves first and foremost as Muslim, Christian, or Jew, the people would identify by nationality. By 1938, when he died in office at the age of 57, it certainly could be said that he had successfully created a unified republic with a common national identity.

The lionization of the founding father of a revolutionary state is a common phenomenon, and usually this is accompanied by a specific doctrine or philosophy. Atatürk's political principles are defined by the "Kemalist" ideology, or more poetically, "The Six Arrows." The standard of the Republican People's Party features a red background with six white arrows displayed in a fan formation. These arrows symbolize the six key canons of Kemalism, which are Republicanism, Populism, Laicism, Statism, and Reformism.

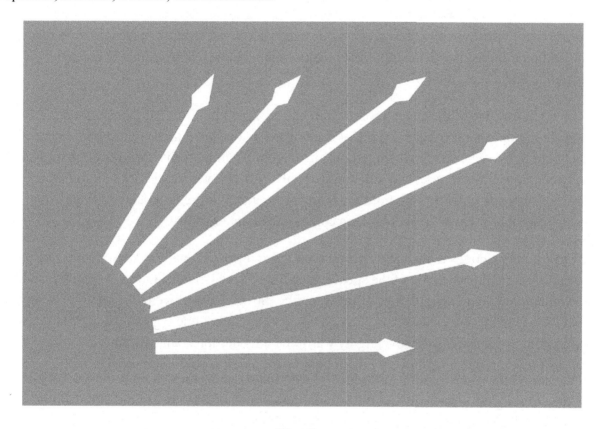

The flag

"Kemal" was the name given to Atatürk by a teacher at his military high school, and such a high accolade could only have come about thanks to exceptional scholarship. It is perhaps an underappreciated aspect of his revolutionary persona that he was widely read, and although largely autodidactic, he was well studied in political philosophy, history, and sociology. Turkish reformism was certainly nothing new, and even under the Ottoman Sultans, reform movements from time to time sought to bring about change, such as the Young Turks. In that sense, Atatürk was not quite as revolutionary as the mythology around him will sometimes suggest. He studied Ottoman history and the great political movements of the age, but he was also familiar with the works of Voltaire, Rousseau and Montesquieu. The charismatic advance of the "Hero of Gallipoli" to power was much more than simply the Machiavellian maneuvers of a good soldier. While Atatürk was a military man first and foremost, he was also a scholar, and Kemalism is a well-founded political philosophy devised by a powerful and original intellect. It was a philosophy of modernization, and this "Turkish Reformation," as it has sometimes been called, demanded a swift transition from a religious to secular state.

Republicanism in the Kemalist lexicon can be defined simply as replacing an absolute monarchy with democratic and accountable institutions of government. The head of state and his governing officials were in the future to be subject to judicial review, and the laws of the land were to be temporal and practical, never subject to the overarching arbitration of God (or those who interpreted God's laws). In conjunction with that, when it came to the details of how the government of the Republic of Turkey was designed and built, Atatürk borrowed from many constitutional precedents to create a unitary state with a single, constitutionally created legislature and a separation of powers.

Populism was one of the undercurrents, framed as a liberation from religious orthodoxy and the embrace of popular sovereignty. Many of the slogans associated with Kemalist populism echoed other similar movements elsewhere, espousing work and national unity, but rejecting class war. Unity counted above all else, and religion, particularly Islam, was ruthlessly subordinated to the state and removed in its entirety from the political theater. With religion thus relegated, it became possible at last to begin forging a common, national identity.

"Sovereignty belongs to the nation unreservedly and unconditionally." These words, attributed to Atatürk, form the backdrop of the speaker's podium of the Grand National Assembly, and they amounted to the founding principle of the Republic. Sovereignty in Kemalist doctrine is simply the unimpeachable independence of Turkey, while at the same time opposing authoritarianism, oppression, and imperialism. Sovereignty was to be unconditional and absolute.

Laicism, as the name implies, dealt directly with the secularization of civil society, removing all trace of religious interference in the affairs of government. This began in 1924 with the abolition of the Caliphate, which was certainly a revolutionary move. The Sultans may well have been retained as a symbolic link to a glorious past, as in the case of many European monarchies, but no such thing was attempted. Secularism was the religion of the Republic, and it was absolute.

Reformism, also sometimes called Revolutionism, simply implied modernization and reform. Ottoman Turkey had, in the years leading up to World War I, acquired the reputation as the "sick man of Europe," and in many parts of Anatolia, conditions of medieval life remained prevalent. The modernization and reforms were thus the most daunting of the six arrows.

Nationalism was the glue to bind the Republic, and a vital component of the revolution. In

Atatürk's own words, "In the administration and defense of the Turkish Nation; national unity, national awareness and national culture are the highest ideals that we fix our eyes upon."

Nationalism was simply the creation of a nation-state from the rubble of an ancient and absolute monarchy. The Kemalist concept of nationalism was informed in large part by the enlightenment concept of a social contract. The Turkish nation, as defined by Kemalism, was "a nation of Turkish People who always love and seek to exalt their family, country and nation, who know their duties and responsibilities towards the democratic, secular and social state governed by the rule of law, founded on human rights, and on the tenets laid down in the preamble to the constitution of the Republic of Turkey."

Atatürk in 1935

When Atatürk died in 1938, he bequeathed a country with strong institutions and an ideology that would chart its course for several decades. Straddling Europe and the Middle East as always, Turkey has been a crucial country in geopolitics, serving as a bridge of sorts between the Arab world and the West. This positioning would lead Turkey into NATO, but in recent years, matters in Turkey have gone in a direction that would no doubt gravely concern its founding father.

In August 2017, Turkey's President Recip Tayyip Erdogan gave a directive to the Foreign Ministry to go into ravaged Syria and rescue an 87-year-old Turkish man stranded in Damascus by the Syrian Civil War. The elderly gentleman lived his life simply and quietly. He disliked drawing attention to himself, and he was grieving for his wife who had just died. The man called himself Dundar Abdulkerim Osmanoglu, but many affixed the title Sehzade ("Prince") to his name, for he was Head of the imperial House of Osman and heir to the defunct throne of the Ottoman Empire.

Osmanoglu was the great grandson of Sultan Abdul Hamid II (1841-1918), who is best remembered in Turkey for introducing constitutional government to the Ottoman Empire after being brought reluctantly to this act by the Young Turks. As this suggests, Erdogan seems to be reaching back to the imperial past, and he appeals more to the authoritarianism of Abdul Hamid II than the liberalism of Atatürk. Similarly, Erdogan's Justice and Development Party opposes the secularism that has dominated Turkish life for almost 100 years. Dundar Ali had never expressed any desire to return to the throne of his ancestors – in fact, he did not wish to leave Damascus, where he had been born and where he worked. It is ironic, then, that a great-grandson of the revolution has reached out to the great-grandson of the enemy of the revolution and embraced his legacy as his own. Dundar Ali now lives in Istanbul, the former imperial capital once known internationally as Constantinople, and interest in the former imperial family and the legacy of the Ottoman Empire is increasing within Turkey, encouraged by Erdogan. There now seems to be a rivalry growing between secularists and Ottomanists, not unlike that which arose between the reformers and the Ottomanists in the 19th century.

Online Resources

Other books about ancient history by Charles River Editors

Other books about Turkey on Amazon

Bibliography

Abou-El-Haj, Rifa'at Ali (1984). The 1703 Rebellion and the Structure of Ottoman Politics. Istanbul: Nederlands Historisch-Archaeologisch Instituut te İstanbul.

Ahmad, Feroz. The Young Turks: The Committee of Union and Progress in Turkish Politics, 1908–1914, (1969).

Aziz Basan, Osman, Great Seljuks, Taylor & Francis, 2010.

Babinger, Franz, Mehmed the Conqueror and his time, Princeton University Press, 1992.

Bein, Amit. Ottoman Ulema, Turkish Republic: Agents of Change and Guardians of Tradition (2011) Amazon.com

Bonner, Michael, et al., Islam in the Middle Ages, Praeger Publishers, 2009.

Cleveland, William L, A History of the Modern Middle East, Westview Press, 2000.

Erickson, Edward J. Ordered to Die: A History of the Ottoman Army in the First World War (2000) Amazon.com, excerpt and text search

Goodwin, Jason, Lords of the Horizons, Vintage books, 1999.

Howard, Douglas A, A History of the Ottoman Empire, Cambridge University Press, 2017.

Kafadar, Cemal, Between Two Worlds: The Construction of the Ottoman Empire, University of California Press, 1995.

Karlsson, Ingmar, Turkiets historia, Historiska media, 2015.

Karpat, Kemal H. The Politicization of Islam: Reconstructing Identity, State, Faith, and Community in the Late Ottoman Empire. (2001). 533 pp.

Kunt, Metin İ. (1983). The Sultan's Servants: The Transformation of Ottoman Provincial Government, 1550-1650. New York: Columbia University Press. ISBN 0-231-05578-1.

Maalouf, Amin, Korstågen enligt araberna, Alhambra, 2004.

Mango, Cyril A, The Oxford History of Byzantium, Oxford University Press, 2002

McCarthy, Justin. The Ottoman Peoples and the End of Empire. Hodder Arnold, 2001. ISBN 0-340-70657-0.

McKay, John P., et al., A History of World Societies, Bedford/St Martins, 2014.

Nationalencyklopedien, NE, 2009.

Peirce, Leslie (1993). The Imperial Harem: Women and Sovereignty in the Ottoman Empire. Oxford: Oxford University Press. ISBN 0-19-508677-5.

Runciman, Steven, The Fall of Constantinople, Cambridge Press, 1969.

Tezcan, Baki (2010). The Second Ottoman Empire: Political and Social Transformation in the Early Modern World. Cambridge: Cambridge University Press. ISBN 978-1-107-41144-9.

Uyar, Mesut & Edward J. Erickson, A Military History of the Ottomans, Praeger Publishers, 2009.

Free Books by Charles River Editors

We have brand new titles available for free most days of the week. To see which of our titles are currently free, click on this link.

Discounted Books by Charles River Editors

We have titles at a discount price of just 99 cents everyday. To see which of our titles are currently 99 cents, click on this link.

Made in the USA
Las Vegas, NV
05 April 2024

88323090R00033